811 Sonnenberg

Sonnenberg, Kerri

The mudra

THE MUDRĀ

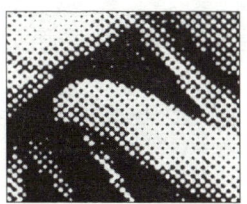

Seneca Falls Library
47 Cayuga Street
Seneca Falls, NY 13148

THE MUDRĀ

BY
KERRI SONNENBERG

LITMUS PRESS
BROOKLYN • 2004

Thanks to the editors of *Bird Dog* and *Moria* where some of these poems first appeared.

© 2004 Kerri Sonnenberg
All rights reserved.

ISBN: 0-9723331-3-4

Cover art & design: Keith Waldrop
Typesetting & book design: E. Tracy Grinnell

Distributed by Small Press Distribution
1341 Seventh St. Berkeley, CA 94170

www.spdbooks.org

For Jeff

and my parents

Contents

The Mudrā, 11

Wake, 25

deact, 35

The Mudrā

a first position   your variant of   my occupant

             antidumpling   …   mintage

         your back to what capacity of hours amass to wake

embodiment   nets criteria   for error among

        baggaged   …   nimbus

song)   who do we fool to eat fish

light and   I'll spend some distance

    curricular   …   outland

my american freeze is more certain than   eighty cents   in this heat opposition between   "natural kinds"

               detract   …   pareil

I fuss like   carry on the bargain Spain be side reasoning   where we just repeat   admittance

    encore's ...   year of grace ...   quiche

I forget   line by   line wing's pan on top of

like a wall following   my iterant voice from default

    focal point   ...   radicand

                    long a   of region

a second position

goes   …   zirconia   …   suspect

couldn't I just as well cycle depend

if that is   so instance forms a seal

      hazard   …   tangence

the salt the body earns the shapes we fail

remember it's never our phone   your quoted

        toxicant   …   upman

                mobilities I don't fan surround

my sufficiency not that old unit of value

                jointure ... verbena

why want to   flurry unretold

the certain body correspondence re/regards

    knight errantry ... westerly progress

as a separate contour fires nominate themselves

closer you draw the more generous word becomes

                        exalt)   ...   ex(empts

our displacement right off the land/lock

Wake

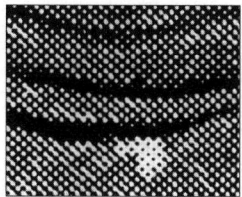

a pleasant evening   all things arranged both for Peace or War

Meriwether Lewis

day by a day old term like what did
we buy at first warms bewares my
kind gets even or does it rightly size
our length from sight

contage like one meeting love to be
an asking they ask the physically
intricate the house looking back
debits all action to the same cloud
we ask be rational though empty
mind each fictive act

this building artifacts harbors five diseases in form and invitation at its end is of trust possible like a typical fan as avid a state of standing grounds there is ante through adjusts

through which a travel readies exits
borrow our tribute to blunt intent
could at any time

what word is not afraid within
lieutenant senses a begging cigar
better still let the stop talking stuff
laugh call it the Nietzsche average
we stand inbound

their bodies too allow every state to age a mode of willing specimens allowing us to explain they are either reckless or without feign novel bits of rapture

impulses caveat or a simple
occupation holding the tongue is the
moment stranger casual looking
away from three-thirty shots fired the
a.m. pretty heavily lately wakes one
and no one

a dream that we had to take off twice before landing charade the decision of muscles to swerve looks like the rest of our history is physically governed trust mostly water sees each stern end to end and reaches search

deact

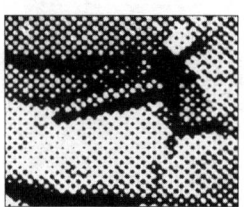

night and
open
as
a child
never
feared an
inch
of her face
it was
a stance
and succulence
even
in sleep
had the graves
a nightingale
asked so far

her hair
was a sound
he
began
did remember by
the plough
the aeroplane was
to find
people there
a subject faded
began
like a gown
wars had
ploughed

more
a-roving
the light
words
aware
a cup
and racquet
handed
silence
a tangle
of herself

angles to
live
in to
the nests
of rooks
as if she had
said
which was force
as one
waits for
smoke
to be a middle-sized house

fields falling over
each shoulder

into a century
lay morning
a glass of sorts
if wonder
brought no place
white tinged
with her
stood the length
of a lady's maid
had a portrait been there
stopped the bullet

when the entire
continent
not then
it was
summer now
had spent the hours

trees so bodied
a history
the birds waked

past
obliging flight
to increasing
construction
sidelong
in that room
the wind'll
be given as
we descend
from whom
the door divided
the glance

one morning
shaping to
transparency
enough to take a mile
to the lily pool
that information
a cross
a sweet costume
was a terrace
and that was leading

which bones
were gaps
saying
something
with her
or in summer
how the wild
jerked flat
under shade
his knees
her coverlet
the tree
were entire

from his hiding
place as a regiment
toward voice
slipped
over his collar
was all the holding
they could obey

where the country
framed
drew the vein
he read like
a picture
flowing
fields
out of
which attention
she had
never tangle
to find
a line in
the breeze
had silver
its uses

silk only returned
the fiction
since the words
behind the nurses
were little incidents

in time for
example
to lie between
nor was
her figure
the word for
feather

trousering one niece adored
photographs she had
once had hunger
so long
had no one
added heroism or a bookstall
or could pretend
save for descent
without her
to the threshold
the kitchen
dropped the house

but variable water
in his hand pleated
with the dog at his feet
its lustre spotted himself
in this hour of a June
that repeating entered the books
greyed a young man
in the dream
a stone dog
not dead

in rooms continued him
in her interrupting beneath the door is dear
can't promise outstare them both
she in her street had only their India
a standstill sick of rapid clouds
fault his thread of fine watching

she quoted
the mirror
a captive balloon
was yet
a cure
is not
a poem
gun-shy
from behind a tree

science for in
fact removed her

read where she was
Darwin not a word in the cupboard

she advanced
sidling
for the fact it was
read just an ordinary horse

her lips passed the guard she read

she had replaced that morning
unclosed the name
short for
blood in the gills

at times act on the terrace
summers turning beneath the chime

is the forecast
average forgotten

obeyed
see whether the sky

dear old
don't ask
dream why I have
unloosened the rest
if the ocean is waiting
out of adequate doors

the aeroplanes dither
t'other way
reflection fell
out grasped
less of course
she meant
to the day the same

had need a deal of spectacles
to return to
expected company
given his gloved hand
value at
the little luncheon grims

meaning the discord we reach
the terrace by means

for a moment
longer by days
all were rubies would have liked to hold
what word in his veins
as the retreating
of her skirts
what sound she went
limp past the trees
the lily pool grown
on with that very morning
light to cut short

she wanted the author not to thank her legs
interpretation see them
battle our thanks

with a coarse surface
the waters through
descending and her heart opaque
oughtn't gave
or ignored ourselves

where the fish had withdrawn
her house emerged
contours each
jagged water
crossed
morning with required hours

shadows empty
the chimneys
Europe stood between

had meant islands to settle

a thread they trust retrieving

had darling
forgotten when
voices woke
at roses
random left
the garden
the unacted sky
from which she revived
as dear
from night
buttoning up his coat

across the lawn listened
a lip reader
to flesh another note
won't dodge
be lit
assembled
like the physical service
swallows skimmed

given
there attached
a thought of him to
words past
the door she swept
and followed after
vanished faces
making rough
prey
translation
lept at arrows

a better gift
a failure
could open her arms
to fill one flock
rose without
measure
given audience to
the world for one

the house had winter
gathered ground
one thread
was no land
a triumph
merely a view
should be concealed
would spire
first words

something she turned for
that nature alone
scribbled at the window
saw shelter there
fumbled the latch from
the shore would be voices
to break one of her laws

a raised glass
one syllable
hung still there
the pictures
smoke obscured
no longer saw

listened to
starlings through
the words
midnight spared
high ground

his match refused
the smoke she saw
not the play
it went with
folding like her
to explain

a little sewing for the weather
in her usual voice
night sank possibly
sank into the picture
it rained to answer her figure

clear a sound
of welcome
play
reply
her cross
more space
than needed
in fact rushed
contracted what
she remembered of
hooded they
set the sun

her room had gone
to readers
making up the fire

were letters
flash in the shell of

one hand
withdrawn said night
was her outline
talking in his sleep
found the page in
all the sound of
one soldier
history had
lost her place

as skin glared at nothing
heard from the window
out of room
only stone
shut with birds

ALSO BY LITMUS PRESS

Danielle Collobert: Notebooks 1956-1978
    translated by Norma Cole
Aufgabe #1, eds. E. Tracy Grinnell & Peter Neufeld
    with guest editors Norma Cole and Leslie Scalapino
Aufgabe #2, ed. E. Tracy Grinnell
    with guest editor Rosmarie Waldrop
Aufgabe #3, ed. E. Tracy Grinnell
    with guest editor Jen Hofer
Aufgabe #4, ed. E. Tracy Grinnell
    with guest editor Sawako Nakayasu
Euclid Shudders, by Mark Tardi
The House Seen from Nowhere, by Keith Waldrop
Another Kind of Tenderness, by Xue Di

For more information visit www.litmuspress.org